Lost and Found

Alan

with best wishes

Harry Greer

Avon   March 1987

by the same author

Arrangements, 1968
The Cutting-Room, 1970
Another Island Country, 1970
Post-War Japanese Poetry, 1972
   (with Lynn Guest and Kajima Shôzô)
The Achievements of Memory, 1974
The Enchanted Acres, 1975
Mountain Journal, 1975
A House Against the Night, 1976
English Poems, 1976
Days, 1978
The Hidden Change, 1978
Zéami in Exile, 1978
Elegies, 1980
Victor Hugo: The Distance, The Shadows, 1981
The Emperor of Outer Space, 1983

Harry Guest

Lost and Found

poems 1975-1982

Anvil Press Poetry

Published in 1983
by Anvil Press Poetry Ltd
69 King George Street London SE10 8PX

ISBN 0 85646 089 3

Printed in England by
The Arc & Throstle Press
Todmorden, Lancashire

This book is published
with financial assistance from
The Arts Council of Great Britain

CONTENTS

ACKNOWLEDGEMENTS

The four poems which appear on pages 32-35 were published under the title *The Enchanted Acres* by Sceptre Press in 1975. Words Press brought out *English Poems* in 1976. 'Brutus in His Orchard' appeared as one of *Two Poems*, Sceptre Press, 1977; in the same year 'Against the Cold' was included in the Oxus/Sceptre Folio/Work in Progress series. 'Equinox', 'Messages' and 'The Embassy of Heaven' were among the poems in *The Hidden Change*, Greylag Press, 1978; Sceptre Press brought out *Zéami in Exile* also in 1978. The *Elegies* were published by Pig Press in 1980.

Acknowledgement is also due to the editors of *Agenda*, *Ambit*, *ASA*, *Atlantic Review*, *Bridge*, *Decadal*, *Divan*, *Here Now*, *Kudos*, *Oasis*, *Outposts*, *Pacific Quarterly*, *Poetry Review*, *Reynard*, *Rock Drill*, *Soma*, *Shearsman*, *South West Review*, *Stonechat*, *Tangent* and *Words Broadsheet* in which other poems have appeared.

In preparing this book I have revised a few of these texts.

H.G.
January 1983

Landscape, Saint-Just

Rock falls sheer to the brown water.
      In one south-facing cleft
bluebells are in flower. A high breeze
      moves in the opposite
larches barely in leaf. We walked
      here in love through still air
to look down on the lily-pads
      though now a cuckoo sounds
hollow across the heath. Beyond
      those Bronze Age monuments —
tall blocks of quartz isolated
      among the gorse — sprawl tombs
from an earlier time dispersed
      and open to the clouds.
Fragile I feel your hand in mine,
      its warmth, until the first
rain-drifts speckle the pond's surface
      with a warning of change.

'A Lane Near Upton'

for R.
25/6/50

I could never find it again.
My diary says
we left our bicycles at the gate
then walked between barley and hedgerow
till we came to the place beneath an oak.
You'd brought your own enchantment
yet the day
matched youth with magic,
lent our love
that sense of a still unencountered world.

Three decades intervene. It proved
the final time we lay in one another's arms.
I search the book of spells in vain.
The skies have changed.
Indifferent seasons sweep the earth. I've seen
the light of sorcery sinking from the fields —
although your face —
its beauty as I kissed it —
stays unforgotten.
I can still smell the fragrance in your hair.

Where the place was
the diary doesn't say — there's just this phrase
'a lane near Upton'.
Bright corn was rustling in a summer breeze,
slow June clouds never hid the sun,
the strip of turf felt smooth, swaying foliage
dappled your bare skin with shadow.
No bird sang and no insect whirred. Once,
a goldfinch passed. All this,
the detailed sweetness, I recall.
Before or after, hours lie in shreds.

The map we used is lost. Memory begins
at a five-barred gate of grey wood.
There were dark nettles and sprays of cow-parsley.
The back wheels went on ticking
when we'd laid the bicycles on their side.
Touching your hand I knew
a sharp foretaste of joy.
The secret quickened in your eyes.

One last caress,
the empty lane,
late afternoon,
the ditches thick with grass —
then nowhere, there's a blank
where sunset should have been,
midsummer harvested and gone,
each signpost wiped out with a rag.
Did we stop our bikes,
linger in twilight,
one foot on the pedal,
one on the tarmac? We must have planned
to meet again, our lips
with their imprint of pleasure
smiling . . . no,
I cannot see that far.
There's no path back from paradise.
The way that leads there has no starting-point.

June 25th, 1980

Hand

I am hand.
There is no sin in me.
I grab what I need —
stem, pebbles, fur.

Angel stricken in the shade
was mine.
The juice was mine,
those curves of fruit.
Wind, mist,
unseizable,
mine too.

Cobnuts are mine,
sweet roots.
I hold the husk, the thorn.
I use an edged stone bright with frost.
My palm bleeds.

I rummage,
probe,
crush woodlice, slugs.
Nothing eludes me.
Fingers scrabble on rock,
inch forward,
reach soil.

I grub up bones.
They stink of then.
I had forgotten.
I'll bury them once more,
scour further.

I am hand.
A smear of red marked yesterday.
The air is still.
His feathers do not stir.
As long as I am I,
am hand,
there can be
no trespassing.

The Embassy of Heaven

The light of sunset
down one side-street
strikes the façade.

Flagpoles
slant empty
over the pavement.

The brass letter-slot
in the high oak door
stays closed.

At nightfall the curtains
remain undrawn. Passers-by
catch a glimpse of mirrors.

Or see through shadowed rooms
to the garden transmitting
a tree in flower

where a building's
transparent heart
baffles the sure.

Lovers

Where are they now, between
what sheets or nowhere do they have
their way? Unwearying
my memories range back whose bright
disturbance brings comfort
in the small hours — flurries lasting
a week, a year, the form
caught sight of, bronze conquest at first
a dream. Calmer after
the sweet effort at times I find
the wrong profile by me
on the imagined pillow — blond
mouth turned to kiss, church clock
striking two, avenue of limes
rustling with moonlight, dark
hands discovering my skin, voice
husky with invention.
Scenes from those days drift past me, drift
on windless plains where ghosts
of loveliness gain shape, disperse.
Where are they now, desires
which harboured me? With the half-light
as ally we made up
such supple contours interlocked.
Do any sculptures carved
by our passion gather cobwebs
in some out of the way
warehouse? My fingers attempting
their salvage have been gloved
in stone. The muscles stiffening
have taken their revenge.
There is no thread that leads past blind
alleys of lust on down
the corridors of remembrance
to where the lovers stand
trapped in the labyrinth of time.

Quercus Pedunculata

There's been a wood here since the last ice age.

Daytime is always twilight,
soft. The branches, swaying, sift
what you think you see
from the perspective of a different world.
Changes occur behind your back
no matter how swiftly you turn.

The glaciers did not reach this far.
To their south the land was treeless.
Cold mist hovered above standing water
and boulders were scabbed with lichen
then as now.
                    The ice withdrew.
Another springtime repossessed the earth.
Men wandered through warmth, through brightness,
hunting the red deer.
Oaks spread, their crinkled shadows falling
over moss and curled ferns and dry twigs.

Air sweeps the high moor.
On cloudless evenings stars
spurt from the north and east.
The mare whinnies to her foal.
New frost glitters.

Here, the river
slides into silence.
Pale trunks distort the slope.
The valley is hidden,
dense with leaves.

You heard no footfall but there's been
a movement over turf
yet what you're staring at is only
space, greengrey, shade-dappled.

Piles Wood, Dartmoor, 1980

Killerton

Grey light is driven from the west.
        The rare flowers lose colour,
lean fluttering against the slope.
        A March wind chaps our hands.
Here there is little sign of spring.
        Song-birds are silent. Day
is a few minutes longer now
        than night but across blurred
fields comes a hint of the late snow.
        With dark glee the children
show us where a dog is buried.
        Rooks fuss in their high nests.
The grass is white with their droppings.
        No one else is abroad
this afternoon save for the ghost
        of a man out walking
his retriever through rain that fell
        a hundred years ago.

Messages

After the yellow lava
has reached the trees in the orchard
twisting them up in a plume of fire
words burden the ear
for what can redeem the fruit-harvest?
But the hand taken and a thumb
gently smoothing the palm,
one kiss, the unkempt hair caressed —
then the demons leave
that were locked in the single body,
and the fears bound taut round the eyelids
start to give. At such times
one statement placed in the silence
"I love you" may be less true
than the fact of skin to skin,
though realler for a moment
than savage photographs showing the torn road,
the farmhouse threatened by molten rock,
the red glare on the skyline.

Landscape, South Dorset

Unclouded dawn. Mist streaks the rose-
      glitter of the Channel.
A hen-pheasant scuttles beside
      one pale lane ascending
the down's sheer green. Under mounds smoothed
      with grass kings lie, their bronze
swords mouldering. The dew is spread
      in silence. Six o'clock
rings from the valley. We came here
      once when the land held less
detail — neither had yet found out
      what the other noticed.
Not that these sites or contours were
      harder to decipher.
Our eyes beginning to focus
      on new textures of love
stayed memory-blurred since they contained
      too many pasts to share.

Against the Cold

I

Soft mask of winter with the eyeholes shut,
the mouth a slack grimace:
                              we watch
its semblance puckered, swelling with the fire
and changing.
The cinders drift to form a dune,
lie flat till the greasy ash
crumbles to powder,
rises as an unsubstantial pillar
and spins itself away to nothing,
falls as haze.

The particles increase,
scurry to the brink
of some achieved design — a map,
the outline of a bird of paradise,
bars of a prison cell.
The breeze stirs fitfully,
unseen fire crackles again
and the scheme such as it was
is nervously erased.

A far-off April rebels
and embers from an autumn strata-deep
disturb it, but the surface holds,
retains the pout of self-deceit.
What was the pattern trying to convey —
a system of geometry perhaps?
the explicit gesture of a god?
Too many plots to overcome it
though few work. So we return
to those high constructions of wet twigs
and a complex grid of canals
with thin and distantly placed bridges.

II

The forest is
November, leaves
cobwebbed with fog.
The rides criss-cross
far apart in
areas of
dripping silence:
soft underfoot
with all the waste
of foliage
brown, fallen — spruce
or the other
dark conifers
merely adding
to the effect
of loneliness.
None can be sure
which direction
leads back from fear.

A horse whinnies
but there's been no
sound of hoof-fall.

In this sudden
clearing stands one
lichen-coloured
fountain never
there before, set
with grey statues
of men and beasts
life-size.
       Behind
a rotting tree
this granite plinth
is wreathed with dead
bryony. Herbs
are stuck upright

in crude glass jars.
A slain bird lies
in the centre,
blue feathers still
sticky with blood.

III

Dark leaden sea
one cloud to wedge
the harbour-mouth
with gold the film
of midwinter
everywhere dun
smoke obscuring
what colour there
once was that picked
each item off
from its neighbour
roof hull chimney-
stack white crates piled
on the quay patch
of lawn glimpse of
distant hill *gold*
breaking become
the same and cold
the wretched cold
of winter weight
of mist to press
all gaiety
forever from
the world without
the *hint of gold*
behind the grey
that bursts as sun
beyond the shroud
that curtains off
one object from
another *blaze*
of gold having
to grope through haze
the blind façades
unlit and bleak
the gardens with
still half concealed
the *radiance*

24

that stars the grey
and shatters walls
of fog until
the winter makes
a heap of drab
fragments lying
underneath *this*
triumphant shine
of final gold

IV

i
Mahogany
reflects her brooch
those dark garnets

her wedding-ring
worn to a thin
uneven wire

ii
Morocco sets —
each shelf displays
a different tone

of leather, black,
olive, snuff-brown
and indigo

Sunlight glancing
off gilt edges
refrains from proof

discarded facts,
old wars, a dead
man's enterprise

iii
Autumn oak-trees
towering by lakes
of glass present

as light floats west
a double mass
of heavy gold

V

A crinkled rectangle
limits the scene —
column of black trees,
ragged flare of sun,
pale green of that receding meadow.
Dusk falls. The gold
withdraws, the wall
seeming to absorb the frame.

Some eerie willpower
keeps the landscape alive
which glows unaltering
long after the real day
beyond the uncovering window
has yielded to night.

VI

Behind the rain an angel waiting,
muscled, wingless.
His bare flesh, rounded perfect limbs
gleam, like a lover's, gold.

A winged cat sprawls lazily
on the turf at his feet.

The rain falls noiselessly
on the discoloured forest,
falls on the far pool knived with reeds,
falls on the yellow slope littered with rocks,
falls here where I wait by the ruined terrace,
falls in the gutted house at my back.

No rain runs off his naked skin
or seems to affect the cat's smooth tawny fur
though my hair is drenched and the cold
downpour trickles into my ears and mouth.

Inside the rain an angel waiting and the sense
of nothing wasted, nothing trivial.
He smiles, for the touch of his outstretched hand
would unshadow time, desire
increase with each fulfilment, spring
be born transparent, hold the world
in one bright weightless moment
and sweep on.

            The rain drives down,
blurs the superb dimensions of the vision,
smears it out. Now nothing
but the usual contours under rain.

Depart without a further glance
at where the magic practically took place.
Depart swiftly with its unearthly gold
stamped on the back of the eye.

For though the symbols of splendour
are one by one pulled down,
there behind each failure,
behind the rhetoric of loss,
behind the spread of winter
and the coils of smoke from charred buildings,
gleams what has been to prove
it may be broken through to once again,
even surpassed.

Communion

for Tasha

'We love we know not what
and therefore every thing allures us.' — *Traherne*

Fourth after Easter. My daughter and I
set out together obeying a bell
in the north tower. Rings of time melt,
travel the speeding vapour of air.
Mid-May. The blossom shaking. We breathe
a far tang of the sea. The sculptured porch
muffles the sound (chime, breeze) as masons
long-dead draw the stone fabric over.
Saints piecemeal round God in glory
replace the sky. Any building, finished,
changes. Altars. Charged with spring flowers.
Books with silk markers. Colours go
from violet round to green — herald the grand
arrival of judgement, blend the three aspects
back into one. Here, touch the future,
tapping the past. At these tables certain
phrases are needed. As is silence.
Also company, you kneeling by me.
We've entered this place so we can peer
inside our hands at questions. Baffled.
Consoled. For mysteries loop, return.

Approaching, chastened, the rail, we reach
a barrier that's been breached between
our fragile pulse-rate and eternity.
Life is offered where amid murmurs
we clutch the fearful permission
to starve. Or feel unscorched the blaze,
rush-past of splendour unmoving. Stand,
not a hair out of place, expectant,
there in the holy cascade — self lost,
though never so wholly oneself. Dear girl,
trust the experience of the jonquil —

30

midwinter's — furled inside black soil —
parched — forgotten — trusting in brightness,
the proper moment. For something tugs us.
Into light. All our knowledge
must be partial. Hear that piping?
The swifts have arrived. Bringing news
from an unseen country. In this life
we face a tapestry hung with the wrong side
always towards us — yet those threads,
the hints of pattern, tantalising, blurred,
are the loose ends of paradise.

The Enchanted Acres

There could have been no time in Eden
merely
       days
when the warmth is a mist of blue and gold
along the blossom beside the fruit
or rain slants
while one five-coloured arch
spans the bruised cloud

       and nights
when starlight detaches each leaf from shadow
the air holds memories of mint and lavender
and drops of water trickling from the ledge
flash into the pool

Beyond the gate
the pulse ticks out its warning.
Trees calculate the loss of autumn.
Suspicious children
compare one pattern with another.
Every white flare of dawn includes
a flavour of remorse.

Back in the lost defended garden
then and now
were pleasures still to come.
There
the heart inscribed
remembrance of the present
while regret
was like blind eyes
when the spectrum throws its glow.

Near Carnac

Smell of hot gorse
and larksong
embroidering the silence.

Far sea glittering
with no horizon
beyond pale dunes.

The stone avenue
lifts along turf to
a broken sanctuary

pointing to sunset.
The grass darkens.
Shadows link stone after stone.

The pile of air above
accepts the change,
the winds of evening,

the chill, disturbance
of a last bird winging home,
eventual starlight.

Magnolias

Curved shell of a soft red petal
on the stone path.
Grey river:
one small craft becalmed
catching the dawn-flush.

Desire alone cannot explain
my presence here, the rage
to hold you naked
before the freezing mirror,
kiss your flesh.

Above, white blaze
of premature magnolia,
motionless,
regal,
starring the boughs,
the silence.

I long for your touch,
for the depiction of loneliness
to glide downstream.

And higher still
another system of twigs
whose scarlet flowers
resemble the parrots of fantasy
perched for a moment
like a sanction
against the unfriendly blue.

Four Hill-Forts

for Michael Bakewell

I

Eventually
grass-green aisles roll down
on nothingness:
here is length light.

Eggardon Hill

II

Conquest:
a darkness brimming
under royal yesterdays.
Careful ascent
seems to lose exactness.

Cadbury Castle

III

History's echo muted
beyond unseen
resplendent years:
flourish
of receding trumpets.

Hembury Fort

IV

More an island —
dunes undulating,
numinous.
Can age
settle these long enmities?

Mai-dun Castle

The Abandoned

A temporary god departing leaves
a blankness to accompany your walk
that falls across green barley, cancelling
brick house-front, sky on elm —
a grace or focus lacking
robs the distance of its light.

A gap in colour measures all that shone
in those weeks when the god strolled at your side:
horizons of stone and nightfall
leaped at the mind's eye, steppes of sun
shook the discovered pastures, you approached
the same lit millpond again,
again.

Now what's beheld is a space dissolving,
ragged ingredients of foliage or cloud
stir at the corners of the glance,
the sounds of May arrive distorted,
the long tombs
send rivulets of darkness over the adjacent crops.

Displacement since that loss
has been recorded in real time;
the causeway you might take on any Wednesday
can never again
echo in that forgotten way beneath your footfall
since the clock commits all trivia to the same
buff file in the same abandoned warehouse.

Gone now forever the frequent gold
that ringed remembrance before it struck.
Withdrawn the god's
bright forefinger piercing the scene.
Failed his enchanted guarantee
that held the next suspended in the last.

Mislaid that formula which led
to gardens out of time
where sprays of blossom hang in azure air
above an unmoving sundial and each kiss
shivers with youth.

Now the insipid waves
lap round an empty pedestal and wash
the faintest hint there may have been a radiance
away.

Gynē

to Lynn

1   The tides shift
in and out
of your skin.

2   You tug at the moon's
orbit with your womb.

3   You know the way
lace ghosts move
through old houses.

4   Eyes gaze at themselves
in every pair
of mother and offspring.

5   Shadows of herbs
brush your fingers.

6   You hold
the young
of each species
roughly
for their own good
and watch
them sleep.

7   Love
contains them
strong as an eggshell.

8   Your milk
lifting along the veins
of April
nourishes
the summer foliage
with light.

9   Silence recalls you
    as the night dissolves
    about your beauty.

10 You listen
    and the unseen attends
    or dream and the unknown's
    remembered.

On the Prescellies, June

for Lee

The most difficult thing
is to stand on the spur
while a late afternoon
unfolds the haze or strikes
the distant lines of hay
and omit nothing, no
note fallen from the high
lark, no grey lamb bleating,
no tang on the faint wind
of clover, the day's warmth,
salt and sheep's dung nor yet
the open taste of air
that has picked up nothing.

A clutter of blue rock,
dark curve of the mountain
lifting towards the east
and the indolent fields
dropping away past green
clumps of oak and hazel —
to record these things now,
not for the future, not
as ingredients of truth
but as lights or textures
deployed round the moment
sufficient in themselves:
that is the hardest task.

A raven flaps its way
downhill and the harsh cry
drags silence behind it.
Small yellow flowers shiver
among tufts of coarse grass
and white stalks pierce the moss
round a patch of cracked mud.

Each detail must be placed
in time — this beetle, two
red moths fluttering apart —
till miles beyond the mist
blurring the plain the sun
lays flat gold on the sea.

Mynydd Preseli, 1978

The Magician's Table

for Tasha

On the ebony worn into grooves
    a cup half full of quicksilver
    the map of the stars of the north
    a raven's skull
    dried rowan-berries in a jar
    a pair of dice whose twelve sides show
            a black crescent moon
            a cobweb
            three diagonal lines
            an eyeless face
            the pawprint of a wolf
            nothing
            two sycamore leaves
            a needle
            a spiral
            an axe head
            a hollow rectangle
            four crowns

If you use the proper words
If you have brought coins of the right year
If you can solve the five questions

Then he will bring out the fragments of magic glass
and place them apparently at random on the table
with none of the small irregular pieces
fitting together in any way

One showed branches waving silently
Another hands on a yellow keyboard
Another numbers written by the dead
Another salt spilling slowly from a tear in a sack
Another someone who walks on sand
Another smoke obscuring a room

Some though inches apart shared the same scene
for a cat might pad across one
vanish
reappear on the other side of the table
and vanish there

He passed his left hand over the fragments
and glass now
reflected only
blackened beams of the ceiling

Three Songs for October

1

Brown water laps
at the abandoned boathouse.
Days grow old. I close
the windows earlier and deflect
those few enchantments inward
stretching parched hands
to the blaze of apple-boughs.

Decline and solitude. Drawn curtains
sadden and piano-music
merely reflects the dark. Tired eyes
to gaze at nothing. Whirr of the clock
and one chime hourly. The chessboard
blooms with dust and a cobweb
trembles between pawn and pawn.

Sparse flowers dry in the vase.
The same admonitory shadows
expand the cold to glass
and wood and china. Tearing up
your final letters I recall
one evening when there were
lanterns across the river.

2

You turn to me and bring
a rhetoric of autumn
                    Voice
that belonged elsewhere
as the weeks here go to waste
the garden falls dishevelled
and past the thorn-hedge
tidal reaches flatten
steelgrey after the gale
                    Your touch
held comfort as the year dissolved
blocked in the space
between the saffron roses
and dangled silence from eaves
now choked with rain
                    Whole memories
of racing sunlight
dropped from your kiss
                    What can
resemble these rooms in winter
where portraits stare at nothing
and where the clock between empty lamps
points to the past
                    A white gull
curves by the gold file of birches
on the landward side
                    The colours
drift and fade
                    An ardour
that descends to tenderness
or worse
            There have been
no messages again
                    Where does
this strip of path lead
under frost

The dark
is gathering in clusters along bare twigs
the way the pool
brushed by the wind starts calm
to collect the night
                The few leaves stir
rasping on the flagstones
and it seems in terror
I have imagined your hand

3

The chain holding the gate to
is brown with rust and a dry vine
lashes it to its post

I walk there once a day
and pick the last of the marigolds

Glance up the lane and see
a tall cloud on the brow of the hill

Nobody comes to revive the year

In wet grass along the hedgerow
the berries swell with venom

The hours lie sterile on each other

Apples fall sour and hard
from branches grey with lichen

No letter from your new address

Rooks drink the twilight
and in the empty house
one stair creaks unnervingly

Moonset and eddies of cold
though nothing moves outside

My face grown pallid in the mirror

Death of a Friendship

I mourn, now that your house contains
such fractured shadows.
This wine you've handed me
tastes sour. I joke and you do not laugh.
When you speak, assuming my approval,
I stare into discoloured
depths of my glass, longing
to get away.

Rain drives against your walls. The few
shrubs you have planted shrink in the cold.
Where there was amity, questions
echo between us. Tufts of dark
lilac branching from tall vases shed
minute dry flowers like grief
for a lost fragrance, leave
on the smooth piano scattered omens
neither of us can read.

The past is empty of romance,
its summers flecked with heartbreak
and its negatives destroyed.
But weren't there moments when
the blue sea glittered, when the lithe
curve of a diver forged another
link between wave and cloud?
I wonder, though, in fear —
were those young grinning faces always
plague-marred, was the fun a lie,
were dreams we've jettisoned
mere husks about this dirt,
dislike? One fiction may
have replaced another for
wherever I look with you I find,
instead of light, a slyness.

We could not name the truth. What used to brag
lies in your cupboard under lock and key.
You care no more
for angels or the underdog,
translating all the terms we used
into intolerance. Your world
now clusters round
the emulation of the rich.

I can't feel glad about old times
because I am afraid
that what I see here I suspected then
but shunned the knowing.
The tarnish of this has rubbed off on me.
The years we shared look counterfeit. If so,
more than affection died today.
What hurts perhaps the most
is that in you as in a mirror shows
not only what I could have been
but what I was or am.

Lady Chapel, Ely

Grey sunshine slanting
in a cube of light.
Mid-May. The paved floor
holds on to winter.

Ferns of dry coral
bleached by the ages
sprout curved and brittle
from fossil-branches.

Clarity fills all
available air
and pushes space back
against the four walls.
The building is steeped
in lore of radiance
cherished, remembered
under the criss-cross
threads of an anthem.

This box of thin stone
presses dark soil while
remaining in touch
with elsewhere. This place
created to track
the flight of angels
acknowledges one
pigeon clattering
by that bright window,
and those who enter
with the right purpose
are borne unwinged past
the places and years.

National Gallery

The forests of another world
    glow on a background mixed
by night — lit trunks, hot foliage,
    each fruit luminous. Sound
comes muffled. Through thin trees, winding,
    one horseman approaches
armed. The blackness stirs as when draughts
    ruffle tapestry. Here
pollen from an unearthly flower
    drifts over vivid glades
making the grass, gold skyline, one.
    Neither picture is ours.
That path leads under the blue threat
    of June. Barley rustles.
Cumulus shadows come, go. Gulls
    cry a warning. The breeze
caught brine, caught soil. The red cliff's edge
    is crumbling year by year.

Encounter

Unseen your skin
with its pleasure
taunted my hands
while long moments
passed in desire
gazing at lips
curved in a smile
and at your hair
catching the light

(Sound of the rain
striking the bright
tufts of apple-
branches in flower
and in the room
reluctantly
day doling out
saffron shadows)

Your fingers were
bound too briefly
around my own
to allow time
for the charming
guesswork of sex
so I stand you
poised in the dream
rose, tanned, naked

Light grows . . .

Light grows and in the stealthy room
      the lovers are revealed —
one full-face, one tanned in profile,
      the eyelid clamped trembling
on both the victories traced by night.
      Soon now, too soon, parting
means the harsh taste of the last kiss,
      beauty locked in mirrors,
bare skin traded for a world where
      lies thrive in sunshine, bronze
statues of triumph in the square
      prance their indifference,
fountains aim at clouds, the lavish
      flowers for sale catch daytime
from the crowd and two who have known
      in secrecy such paths
along each other's pleasure must
      tread pavements as strangers.

Equinox

The hills
tug at one another
capped with beech

A pared moon swings
uncanny
in the copper sky

Each blade of grass
is now a magnet
and the dew
falls as sparks

Ears of corn
silver beneath the soil
begin to sway

The bedrock
sings with tension
and a pebble
held to the cheek
whines

The air splits in two

Out through the new
fissures of darkness
tumble the rose
the pear
the hard holly

There is one clap
of bright
inaudible thunder

The night closes
sealed

Earth has crossed
the threshold of summer

Advise Me

You sit up late
in your house on the estuary
    while the thorn-hedge
    sparks into flower
and cold stars swirl about the tip
    of The Bear's tail.

    Ten years. Ten years
without you when I think at one
    now legendary
    time five minutes
apart would have been too long dragged
    from your kisses.

    You re-appeared
out of some unmapped place. Poems
    describing you
    went humming round
those grey concrete walls. You were still
    slim, still charming

    as when pressing
against me, eyes moist, you'd pleaded
    with me to stay
    but lust is such
a fickle master I stood close
    by you unstirred.

    Drink wine alone
for night flattened on your windows
    will not betray
    secrets we shared
and treasure still although we own
    them no longer.

Near Avebury

Beyond the field one block
rears taller than a man.
The lichen makes green stars and noon
scoops at the surface with shadows.

Ripening corn
flows past the plinth of turf
where furrowed soil
bordered the dry
stalks of January.

Bright axe,
the flakes of healing leaves,
antlers,
jet bead —
what mysteries were found
gripped by the skeleton?

Along this hedge
note the convolvulus,
whitened,
dying.

Document

I changed my flag and fought against
    the stars, but still you haunt
me with your dark hair, with your blond
    hair — not have I forgone
allegiance to a time when each
    white bud unfolding meant
a catch in the throat mimicking
    desire. The foreign braid
glittering on this uniform
    proclaims my loyalty,
conceals the cost — an ageing heart
    in conflict with itself.
I walk beside this canyon where
    grass-blades on the further
lip show gold in the setting sun
    for fate baulked of her prey
confuses what I glimpse beyond
    with boredom, with longing.

History/Prehistory

Pelléas and Mélisande

They met in the shadowed garden.
                    Between the trees, far off,
lay the last of the shining water. It was
their first encounter. They were alone.

Cries from the crew and the great
                    sails hauled aloft. Brightness
withdrew from the high gold span of day.
Hissing against the waves the ship entered

a stormy sunset. A lighthouse blinked.
                    The castle, her new home,
unseen. Only the one glimpse of sea. Elsewhere
dense tree-trunks, vines, flowered shrubbery.

There were no words as darkness thickened,
                    leaves swayed and a salt breeze
brought the cold. And still she did not move
looking through twilight at her husband's brother.

St Juliot

Thomas Hardy, Monday 7 March 1870

A stile of vertical blue slates,
ferns licking them.
The churchyard starred with snow,
still falling.
Scrawny daffodils bent
over a cast of snowdrops.
Steep field.
Below, a steeper wood,
leafless, sleeving the torrent
tumbling, tin-grey.

Snow blown from the south,
bruised wall of sky.
Flakes circling an unseen centre.
Snow through bare thorn,
lying as powder on the flat primrose leaf.
Snow in the gale hissing among branches.

Beyond the wind was silence.
Then the boy coughed and the door creaked open.
The nave was cold where the girl prowled,
read the carved tablets with no excitement,
turned to her parents again,
smiling, impatient.
                        Who would not swap
wisdom for youth, being middle-aged,
yet have traded firm thighs for understanding
in our spring years?
In this place once regret was focused.
The splendour here was celebrated late,
perhaps not even recognised as splendour
till the chance was gone.
What mapped then — think, compare — our meeting?
A chalk lane and a shingle beach,
the cropped grass of the high down,

far glitter of the sea . . .

He came here alone
with the green beginning.
Flowers sparked among the gorse.
There was salt in the north wind.
He came expecting nothing
and what was there he did not see
until long afterwards, again alone.

The vision, elusive along these lanes, was irony.
When he re-visited the place and found
even her ghost a teasing absence, all
he had ever written about tricks life played
seemed cruelly confirmed
near the waterfall and at the turn in the path.

Gusts bring more snow. It's time to leave.
Our son sings to himself and our daughter
asks questions ignoring the answers and we nod
and try to explain, holding chapped hands,
laughing together,
not without reverence, no, with awe
at such wry gifts, at that
embittered passion, at the waste,
the grief remembered and the love
known at the wrong time and set down too late.

At the Tomb of Chateaubriand

He recommended
a blunt grey
cross stuck here
against the north.

Green sea
hisses beneath on granite
and the unceasing
gales bring mist.

Under the stone slab
a fleshless head
stares into earth.

Ear-sockets
of crumbling bone
catch the pointless
noise of the living.

Nothing excludes
the tide's return
or the black wind
or the seagull's
questioning cry.

Saint-Malo, April 1978

Zéami in Exile

for Keith Bosley

The Nô poet Zéami, banished to the island of Sado in 1434, is reputed to have written there one of his greatest plays, Yuya, the story of a courtesan made to dance for her lord even though she has received news that her mother is dying in a distant village.

Wild island
and the north too near.
I walk among sparse colours
hearing the gulls cry above the rocks.
Endless the black foam-covered waves
that bar the gulf.
Through far haze sometimes
I glimpse the mainland,
blue mountains where the road
starts for home.

Impulses spurt in the heart —
old plays danced by brocaded actors,
court-ladies veiled in perfume,
the ache of distance.
What crime, what fault, what slight?
Displeasure and the lord's command.
The journey here, brightness dwindling.
Silence
after the salt crash of history.

The fishing-boat is a speck in cold sunlight.
A hawk grabs something out of the sea
and dropping it again
screeches, wheels.
I alone
not free to leave
this island that hangs in the sunsets of other men.

I pace the shore
spattered by spindrift,
murmur my prayers
in the smoky hut at nightfall,
wait for news.

And the gift falters.
A plant uprooted at the wrong time,
fixed in another courtyard, shrivels,
dies. My brush
suspended over this coarse paper
is laid down again.
The gale tears at the shutters,
flecks the ground with snow.
I read. Outside,
the empty speed of air,
the cold like cruelty in the mind of power
and the classic texts
do not spring into images,
offer no song,
no pattern.

Days change into one another.
I visit the shrine,
rinse my chapped hands,
stand by the vacant gate.
Or, in the frozen gloom of the temple,
repeat the proper words, eyes downcast
like the saviour's. He said,
The house is on fire for threescore years
and still we are reluctant to escape.

Bright ghosts tug at the sleeve. Tall grass
hissing in the palace garden.
Memory wears a painted mask,
speaks with a borrowed voice.
Lost passions drifting
as light depends on autumn or a stone
is dropped in the quiet river.

66

Darkness arrives and the wind
pours unabated from the sea.
A letter perhaps.
From an old woman.
Ill, far away and by herself.
The daughter pleads in vain
but has to dance.
Flowers tremble on the cherry-trees
and she weaves the call of conscience
into the dance, her steps unfaltering,
longing to be gone.

A light shower falls along the branches.

The brush
makes shapes down the damp paper,
each line
spreads sideways to the next
blurring the picture.
Cooking-smells from the brazier
sting my eyes and nose.
The waves
smash against the twilight
and I shiver in the gusts that jog the door.

Rain then on the fragile blossom.
A few petals fall, the dancer
catching them on her open fan.

And does the lord relent?

Memories of the Sinagua

When the mountain thundered
    and black ash hid the light
our people fled the anger of the gods
    ran with their blankets and pitchers
ran till far ahead a line of sky
    turned dark but not with smoke
darkened with night and there were stars
    stars only opposite those fleeing faces

When dawn yellow as a flower showed
    in a wider line of sky the roof
of smoke seemed thinner and not so dark
    nor was the roar of the mountain so loud
nor did the ground keep shaking under their feet
    shaking as they ran so that children stumbled
and the old had to be supported in their haste
    while the mouths of all gaped with fear

Our people came to the bank of a river
    a small river sluggish and winding through bad lands
where the water often failed in the hot season
    and no one could save the stalks of corn
that withered and rattled in the dry wind
    without coming to ripeness

But there was nowhere else to go for the smoke
    covered the sunset and at night
distant flames flickered in the darkness
    while beyond the river that became our river
the many-coloured bad lands spread
    where nothing grows and the soil is poisoned

There was no other place so our people remained
      digging the pits in which to build houses
growing cotton and jointfir and green beans
      and many died in the parched times
when there was no river and the sky cloudless
      and the ditches cut through our fields held dust
though we sacrificed deer to the gods of the place
      and danced beating the soles of our feet on the earth
as rain beats down from the fat white clouds
      so corn can grow tall and the saltbush make its seeds

Our fathers and their fathers kept watch
      while the mountain spat fire
and the darkness that was in the sky
      dropped on the ground so that too was darkened
turned dark as the black ash dropped and lay thick
      till the land they had known as a good land
sloping red and ochre away from the mountain
      became a black land that was soft in its blackness

And then we are told the mountain fell silent
      the flames died the ash stopped drifting
and the sky cleared the way the wind
      combs away smoke over a cooking-fire

Seasons passed with rainfall and snow on the mountain
      the land stayed dark and silent beneath the wind
and our fathers saw green shoots on the blackness
      wondering they saw flowers
speckling the soft blackness like blue stars
      marvelling and thankful for the gods had sent them
had sent them flowers as a sign the ash was good ash
      sent flowers to show it was time for us to return

Our buildings stand sturdy and square and red
        the corn grows high and green in the fields
our women weave bright clothes from the cotton-plant
        our granaries are filled and our men squat at leisure
throwing their gaming sticks on the hard floor and shouting
        while scarlet birds screech that are brought by the traders
from a land to the south where such birds are common
        flashing their plumage in a place of many trees
for here a man may hunt all day with his dog
        and see no more trees than his hands have fingers

We are safe at the foot of the silent mountain
        tilling black earth and watching the breeze
drive a black haze over the fields
        for summers are dry now and the dust
lifts and spins taking the form of a wraith
        that runs dark and shapeless in front of the wind

Note *In A.D. 1065 a volcano erupted in northern Arizona, driving the Sinagua people from their settlement. When the eruption ceased it was found that the layers of ash had made the ground more fertile than before. The Sinagua returned and farmed the land successfully until in the thirteenth century a long period of drought forced them to leave the area forever, though the splendid ruins of their villages still stand in what is now desert.*

The Sisters

Luke 10. xxxviii

One sat in wonder while the other
went to the well,
fetched oil and salt from the storehouse,
dropped plates, scolded the cat,
chose wine in jugs, set fruit out.
And no one
crossed the tiled floor of the kitchen,
nor at first
did she ask for help,
just muttered underneath her breath
and felt hard done by.

The cat climbed in the visitor's lap
and Mary listened to the wry
glowing account of the way all things could be.
For food and drink
at this one time
were of no account.
Hospitality
for once
lay in the ear and heart,
not in business or display.
They were for later.

Images of Christmas
for Nichol

The tavern yard. And snow.
A heap of broken jars. Rakes leaning.
Stone trough bearded with icicles.
A disused shed,
laths showing through the plaster.
Inside, the mother in the hay
and Joseph, hand to chin, watching
while she attends to songs from another world.
Angels stand daylong on the peeling thatch.
The ox stirs,
the ass stamps a grey hoof
and the stable cat yawns in the straw.

God is a baby
and these stars, this frost
glitter forever at the core of time.
A king is born of a realm that has no name.
A priest is born who gives
transparent as a window on to truth.
A victim is born
to hold in wounded hands
the doom of all who suffer, all who die.

Three sovereigns kneel by the manger.
Dazzled, uncomprehending,
they lay down their gifts —
gold for the king of a land without frontiers,
incense to wreathe the priest who walks
as simply with the dead as with the living,
gold for kingship,
incense for prayer
and ointment ready for a sacrifice.

Bells ring in the unbuilt cathedrals.
The holly sways in the trackless wood.
And candles light the way to leave
the dark in any year.

Brutus in His Orchard

Lull in the storm. Between these walls
a sense of time mislaid.
No moon.
The constellations blurred by cloud.

The trees hang heavy in the dark.
An owl's note shivers from the distance.
Drenched grass. Spread cobwebs here and there
catch at the glimmer of a falling star.

The hours drift to a standstill.
Night. And somewhere. Does the way
lie in this direction,
that or this? And dawn's
grey knifeblade at the east
behind which branch
leafless, invisible?

Meteors pierce the mist,
leave red tracks on the sky.
The cold air apprehensive
and the compass gone.

Far thunder.
                    Still
the time seems ripe. And death
at this extinguished moment
logical, not to be feared.
A step towards oblivion.
No more.

I am not I. And nowhere. Am
a process of thought
lost in the darkness, dark mind
without position, past or action.

Inside the night. And by myself.
What I must do is harm. Now.
Either way.

A light.
The boy approaches.
Perhaps a message or reprieve.
The wind gets up once more, some rain
spills on my hand and I'm
no longer quite alone.

Antinous

His beauty stands between two worlds.
　　　We picnic here on scraps
from private islands, half sunlit,
　　　half in shadow. Hadrian
banqueted. Live flesh absconding
　　　bequeathed the emperor
nothing but a dream of youth, sweet
　　　sweat, bare echoes above
the great river. Statues began
　　　kindly imitating
the past. In vain. Can a chipped mouth,
　　　blank eyes, the block of throat
dovetailing awkwardly with robes
　　　of stone, convey the loss,
that alien fragrance needed, gone?
　　　The drowned don't pose. Tribute
frequenting empty rooms is no
　　　match for the vanished kiss.

A Sense of the Past

Two eagles in a cleft of the sky above Delphi.
We trod rough grass in the stadium.
Thrasydaios the swift boy ran here
praising Apollo. The centre of the world is close.
Immortal light fell on the victor's limbs, his hair.

History of Art

Art
like alchemy
waits for the full harvest

Smooth wheat
flowing pale and silent
into the storage jars

The smith with scorched hands
tempers the hot bronze
and the masked priest
dances amid fiery leaves

Leisure to trace
the twig across wet clay
and see each thing for what it is
as well as what it does

Whine of a swan's wing
across the flat spaces of the estuary
or sudden
orange on the swerving kingfisher

Watching till waves
cover the thorns of limestone
or adapting the night sky
into triangles and legends

When the grain is threshed
and the fruit gathered in
when the animals have bred
and the stockade's been secured
then images may be carved
of a world that never was
and the bright deer painted

Now is the time
to mix lead with sulphur
and from the cooling ash
draw the dry useless gold

Grave-Goods

Spain, c. 29,000 B.C.

They stayed in the shadow of the overhang
to watch him die.
There was no room for grief,
barely enough for a grave.

He gazed past them into daylight.
They were only shapes that stood,
presences without feature.
And in their stillness they knew —
even he had to obey that quick
choking, stop of the heart.

He would soon be a part of them.

His eyes lost life as the sun
reddened the far side of the valley.
A wolf howled close to the cave.

The elder son cut off the head,
scooped out the brains.
All ate solemnly
for he had read the scrawls of lightning,
set broken limbs,
found hidden water.

Apart from him they were afraid.

The pit was shallow.
Bending down they laid
his stone knife, still bloodstained,
across the ragged neck.
Then the dog-fox and the ewe were slain.
He would need patience as well as cunning
stumbling among the dead.

Mixing ochre into the soil
they heaped it over his wasted body,
over the slack animals,
over the knife he had made.

They returned to the cave each autumn,
chipped fine blades and hunted,
built fires.

Then they did not return.

The valley
thickened with trees.
Centuries were measured
in rainfall and avalanche,
the movement of herds.

Then others came,
took shelter in the narrow cave.
His spirit was strong.
They lived there many seasons,
tiptoed past the mound,
and left it untouched.

Lithuania, c. 6,000 B.C.

When she was dying
they lashed her legs together.
She must not be allowed to walk.
They had all seen those who were dead
loom threatening like strangers.

A stone axe lay under her neck.
Between her knees was a bone dagger.

The boy pointed at the dagger.
When she stirred again, after the death-cold,
her fingers, groping for it through loose soil,
could cut the thongs that tied her.

The man nodded
and fetching more strips of hide
bound her wrists.
Straightening up
he spat on his hands
and cast the necklace of boar's teeth
into the pit beside her.

Hastily they scraped the earth into a pile.
Her skin seemed to flinch.
When it was all covered
they gazed at the mound in fear.
Her eyes
were pressing against the dirt
striving to see them, the buriers,
those who were still alive.

Muttering words that had to be said
they backed away.

Mist hovered by the lake.
The hillock with its raw mound stood empty.
She lay there, trapped, newly dead.
The air above
quivered with curses.

Brittany, c. 2,300 B.C.

Using bracken and thorn-branches
they swept the floor of the chamber.
The dry stone blocks, carefully fitted,
gave off a smell of earth.

The narrow entrance allowed
a far-off flicker of the sea.
Wind hissed over grass,
brought fragrance of gorse and hawthorn.
Inside the tomb the air was still.

It was time for the offerings.
One box made of oak
held bronze axes. Another,
flint arrowheads. Another, made of elmwood,
was crammed with daggers.
All were unused.
A ritual wound nicked each blade.
They too had died.

When the gifts were in place
the tomb was sealed.
They buried the chamber with clay and pebbles,
roofed it with turf.
Time in utter darkness
slithered between the boxes.
The captive air grew stale.
There was no sound —
save from time to time a chink of bone
as the skeleton fell apart.

English Poems

The easy daylight . . .

The easy daylight
unrolls over soaked farmland,
cold stain of ponds
edged by the leafless alders.

Unmapped perspective
whenever the crinkled steel
of some unlikely river
seems too close.

Beyond the tall shadows of the winter
where sunlight is loosed
in green and dark mirages and in cloud
a hint of snow-flurries far away
is leaning against
the enigmatic hills.

Stand close and dare to disbelieve . . .

Stand close and dare to disbelieve
in the ghosts of departure.

I hear your breathing measure what remains,
a stir of dust behind the photograph,
the stone steps by the terrace
preparing their echo.

Sundial and urn
continue their disintegration,
months of your anguish
shred into the dark.

All we committed here
hangs in the growing shadow,
trails at our heels throughout
the time to come.

Rose light and the westering day
suffuse the clock face. Hold my hand.

Chalk escarpment . . .

Chalk escarpment
and the buried river.
Lost ritual —
the braided cloths along the bank,
the sun's disc sliding in pails.

Picks formed from elk-horn
littered the dry valley.
Brambles, a scooped-out quarry,
flash of a green snake
and a smell of spark around those flints
like glass.

Here in the morning light
stand on the sea-bed
while the frail
skeletons of extinct creatures
come drifting down.

Summer is once again . . .

Summer is once again
my inability to love,
an empty table in the window
and readiness for scorn.

Who can survive among
these pyramids clipped from box
or peacocks spreading dark foliage
down narrow alleyways of turf?

The marjoram succeeds
and songs of triumph
are shaken from the lilac.

And if I chose
to turn the fountain off,
lock up the herb-garden
and the peach-trees?

Abandoning starlight
and the heavy scent of earth
to memory or
the incessant rustle
of the hour-glass.

Never again . . .

Never again
to see this length of water
or the fields
descending from the distance
to the further shore

White sails
on the tides of April

We turn indoors
to the bedroom full of photographs

One evening ahead
to start unfastening
the thorn-shoots tethering us here

Faint gauze
passes across the sun
and I watch you in the looking-glass
for the last time

Precarious touch . . .

Precarious touch
as often before
on the iron cord
bracing conscience.

Four metal pennants
hold the prevailing wind.

The limestone buckles,
swells. The tower
impenetrable on the sunrise
poises against collapse.

All too soon
releasing from the crypt
such whiffs of resolutions
long concealed.

Reddish nets ...

Reddish nets
dry on the harbour-wall
where spheres of pale glass
put off the sunlight.

A trail of smoke
from the departing ferry
hangs in the sky.

I leave the deserted quay
hearing the seagulls
and cross the intricate
reflection of the town
in the wet sand
composing the first of many
unanswered letters.

Night thins along the vault . . .

Night thins along the vault
and praise
tugs the reflection
blue and gold
along tomb and stall
and kneeling figures
in cloth or marble

You are here
though you won't believe me
via the force of love

Silver morning
tentatively
highlights finger
and open book

The altar
stands out from emptiness
fresh statements in a bygone language
inhabiting the ear

Woods dense and the old . . .

Woods dense and the old
brick buildings hidden.
Roar of continued
water, path and trees
in an unseen mist,
a dank smell hanging
on the windless air
like iodine. High
walls run from the house,
enclosing a dark
garden blocked by one
yew-tree. Neglected,
a long lawn shows yards
of daisies, plantain,
its borders always
in shadow where flowers
fight the way noon mutes
them all save one white
lilac with such shapes
of blank fragrance that
momentarily
assert the summer.

The god has entered the sea . . .

The god has entered the sea
like a spread darkness
although my skin
is dazzled from his touch.
Elements of air and landscape
are one by one ticked off —
the samphire, hollow in the sand,
curve made by a grey gull on the wind.
The world brought down
to the sound of night,
to recollections of what thrilled
and therefore is discarded.
I apply
the acid-test of dreams
and am left with
strange detours round the past:
transcriptions, five-
finger exercises,
the shadow of a kiss,
one colour and the blemished gaze
from an ironic looking-glass
stuck in a previous year.

Winter . . .

Winter.
The lamplight.
Black third-floor panes.
My thigh beneath your hand.
The portraits avert their eyes.
We commit love.

Nemesis.
Can thought bring on the end?
Old stone flaking.
The roof glistens under dew.
Thrush-song and a May sunrise.
I leave your tousled bed.

Desire is where you would have been . . .

Desire is where you would have been,
love where you are.
Shock of his mouth on me,
the cornfield stretching round us,
and his sudden taste. Daylight then
span with stars as the texture of July
clung to our palms; bared skin;
caress. With those forgotten hills
jutting above the dry gold stalks
dark on the west. First
ebbing of the summer and the boys
get up reluctantly, stare
at the altered fields their eyes
wild with a silver focus, dress,
walk hand in hand across the frontier,
kiss once again more absent-
mindedly than to confirm, gaze back
at the lost enchantment under cumulus
and we are pledged forever you and I
to that long private look at that
receding memory. Desire's a land
you think you visited,
love solid ground.

Romance . . .

Romance
A table-top littered with amethysts
Your hand on the faded map
deciding

The islands again
Dark leaves
strewing the inlet
And the memory of you
standing naked
in the tumult of summer

The firelight trembles and the gale
shakes in the chimney
Your eyes elude mine
though your kiss
was shot with salt light

Those cliffs relinquished by the sun
and the purple flowers dying

Chill sand
beneath bare feet

The imagination of your love

High leaves on fire in the evening light . . .

High leaves on fire in the evening light
The valley blurred with gold
Dark lilac casts
a shadow on the stream
Silence
Save for your presence
hawthorn, may,
beside me
We talk intermittently
of the fading day, your hands
the shining grass
and in your too briefly
repeated glance
the way the dying east
withholds its stars

You haunt the orchard . . .

You haunt the orchard
and the telephone
kindles your silence

The greengage bowl, clothes
you once wore, comment
of the dark hillside,
vetch and pimpernel,
the locked desk, one book
with the place marked and
a dried-up inkwell

You once said when we're
older dreams between
embraces would go
but recollections
throng the deserted
galleries and warp
pure lines of the stream

Banish your shadow
and the willows shed
their silver
                    Love once
more and your return
naked, indifferent,
through mist, through autumn

Sound of the weir against the distance . . .

Sound of the weir against the distance,
clematis
starring the grey wall

The black tom cleans itself on the top step,
pauses as a bat starts hunting

The landscape adjusts to twilight
gilded by air that flows
from the slopes of legend

Paragraphs of the past
ablaze with woods left by the axe,
untouched parks strolled through,
love never spoken

Beneath lost colonnades
those lips not kissed
kissed hard and again

The sunset draws the evening away
and colours now diminishing
turn cold

November afternoon . . .

November afternoon
The first frosts
I remember
your body underneath my hands

These spare boughs
separated by mist

Few gold leaves

Deer pick their way
over the hard grass

The clock
painstakingly
works through the white day
as I move in wonder
further from you
wherever you are

Stained sunlight . . .

Stained sunlight
falls through prayer
dry sand
crumbling past shadow

Agreement whispered
and the time-dark pew
reaches through granite
to the scarlet winter
touching frost

Jackdaws spilled wheeling
where the half-hour
collides with dawn

Stone lilies
and the immobile
angel's wing

The mutter of lost hours
and dead hands
in harmony
smoothing the page

Victory

Kneel on the cold
so many lines of soil
above the past

Each vantage-point a memory of love . . .

Each vantage-point a memory of love
once shuttered houses open to the day
and the dead sit there contentedly
in armchairs warmed by the falling sun

The stone goes yellow, holds the heat
this side of darkness where
I invoke you
                    By the pool
the rhododendrons withdraw their bloom

Love meant for evening
questions each former kiss
with dreams of re-discovery
                              The voices
plan delight
              Or else rejection

You opened the piano, smiled and played
The window indicates a moon,
black roses
                    Cry of a nightjar
The distant church counts nine

Furniture, velvet, leather bindings
show best by candlelight
Your profile now transparent
trembles, departs

Cupped hands . . .

Cupped hands

Gold water brimming

A kestrel hovers
somewhere in the depths

Slow clouds passing
miles below the backs of my hands

The magic trembles
and the colours out of time
tarnish

Open the fingers
and spill forever on the ground
what seemed to be

Elegies

The First Elegy

The area was overgrown. Brambles and fireweed
had to be uprooted before a boundary
was agreed upon and the last pale
driven in next to the first. Sometimes
the acreage is complete before pen touches paper,
at others the map only remains itself and the final
shading contradicts the outline made at the start,
for example a grey summer's day and on the lake
hardly waves only the slightest folding
over of water on water with nothing reflected
though the hills enclosing it were purple
and on three sides trees came down to the shore.
Adults were elsewhere. We skimmed stones or sat round
in the gritty boat-house. What furniture I remember
appears scoured and cheap. There was a gramophone
playing swing. Unheard mosquitoes
stung our bare legs. Today we stroll beneath lime-trees
in another garden that does not belong to us.
At that time we could not have known each other
even though in a sense sharing the same time-zone,
privation, absence of sunlight, for war
had removed our fathers. The faces are unlabelled,
those melodies possess only a period texture.
I cannot recall who owned the property nor where
we went later. There was a small rocky island
but no boat and I couldn't swim in those days.
The dramatis personae were children on their own
for an afternoon and you and I increasingly
find ourselves left behind as they run over stubble
where the last swallows flash or enter gloomy
chambers in some ruined castle where the lintels
are too low for our foreheads. But a chipped stone egg
on my desk admonishes me for change

emerges from the air and colours the thinnest
depictions of the past. Late June there. Few flowers —
the one rhododendron flecked with unclenched scarlet
shows by its listlessness it has fulfilled
a yearly duty. The blinds are half drawn though only
on one far field where the hay has been cut
sunlight, slanting, picks out yellow among the green.
Knowledge of being alive at a given moment —
given if not taken — has details of heat and shrubbery
absorbing the past tense before we exclude them.
On the ground floor, there in the room forming the corner,
two oil-paintings, each about the size of a postcard,
display these illusions: one, a path through a wood in spring,
the other, a slow stream broadening into pools
under brown foliage. Both show what was needed
though neither comments on anything here
since the brush-strokes limit the scene not for the viewer
only but for the dead painter himself.
The way they've been hung would imply that it's the second
picture that holds autumn replacing April.
It could though be the other way around.
Take a day, any day, says the old fortune-teller.
It may be one that rises with indifference
to the surface, flicks the merest hint of a red
fin, gold scales, one among others, but at that time
you sat and read or went upstairs in a house
that has since been destroyed. You showed me the place,
now asphalt, near the church we were married in.
A copper beech spreads over this wall
and the dead elms show stark amid all the green.
When you were ascending that stair you saw
floor-boards stained dark, a carpeted edge of landing,
no foreshadow of a wind with dust and fumes
blowing across a sunken highway or its intrusion
years later into our talk. You stepped into space
going perhaps from one high room to another

and the crunch of gravel is cancelled under
our shoes as we leave this path for the lawn
but where I wonder will the two of us be when this
is remembered together or separately. The sun by now
has closed the last of the distant hay-fields though one
shaft of light sinks through green water in the estuary.
The open sea is concealed by the long shoulder
of the foreland. In theory you can walk round any lake.

The Second Elegy

Locality is present in the curve of a bowl
and the style has lost all heritage, all sense
of place, gone nameless, international.
Geology though cannot be flouted and subtler
changes happen in the quality of clay
even from village to village. The water, pigment,
wood-ash, flowing through space, reach time. It is hard
to detect lost sunlight or lines on the potter's hands
but soil round the roots of the plum-tree still
matters when fruit is eaten miles from the farm.
Some years ago now, on a walking holiday,
I encountered the whereabouts of a ghost.
At a threshold in the centre of the manor-house
you moved three centuries. The owner's voice
went on explaining but now there was a sweet
illness in my nostrils that got stronger
as we mounted the stairs till in the narrow
bathroom overwhelmed I had to lean on the cold wall
hearing words with difficulty through a smell
of rotten flowers, vase-water, meat going off,
and it was there according to the legend
that the dead monk had lain. There are also
the books to be chosen when one is about to cross
a desert. It is important to know something of the rocks
as well as the living things — rare blooms, the snake
coiled to strike — for there are bound to be lodestones.
Before selecting compass and penknife
one is strongly recommended to make a note
of one's own name and address, even mark the house
on the map for mirages occur and time-slips
and people have been known to stray far from the dusty
water-courses. No one belongs in an airport.
We motored over with rugs and a wicker

picnic-hamper to watch the fragile 'planes taxi
on the flat grass. Mechanics and travellers seemed
to have a place there but then that was an aerodrome.
We lay together at the foot of the slope discussing
desire in whispers, the dew was tracking the sun
as it diminished, the busy or languid players
cast distorted shadows on the field and the bat
struck the ball a full second before the sound reached us.
You watch lightning flicker over the tossing trees
and count five spaces of time as one mile. Today
the bar of twilight stretched between pole and pole
travels as fast but we adjust our watches
without winding them. Many have died since that time
and I have mourned them, attended the funeral,
grieved for the unseen smile, the dependable love,
but then dry seeds dropped in the earth give no
indication of stalk or flower, no glossy
berry or flourish of leaves, if a pun is not flippant
there is no hint of the yew-tree, indeed
looking at a corpse one would say, This is nothing.
The soul has begun its journey. You listen
to a record with the cat on your lap, the sounds
pass her unheeded. We also fail to intercept
movement of angels or the clamorous sense
made by the dead we knew. Other examples
demonstrate time — petrified sea-shells clinging
to the mountain-top, cold accumulations
of lava carved by the endless wind. A grouse
scuttled over the heather and I searched
for the nest without finding it. Unseen, always,
the wonder of speckled egg, of shrivelled leaf
and the seed-case is matched by the wonder
of fossil and rainbow. This is the interchange
of faith and belief. A sandstone escarpment
drops almost sheer to the north. Far below
in the green cup scooped by ice is a round pool

and sheep are grazing. In better weather
you could see more but at noon sudden spurts of rain
blur even the near-distance and grey shreds of cloud
pass level with the summit. It is politic
to keep out proper names as far as possible.
Poems aren't works of reference. They provide
the interested reader with the kit he needs
for an excursion into the uncharted hills
from which he'll come back tanned, unfocused, acquainted
with other ways of expressing each pavement or garden.
And there are as many editions of poems
as there are readers because *house*
will have a different shape for each of us
and *apple* a different taste. What do you see
when the word *red* is mentioned — bricks, a cock's comb,
the Whitsun altar, part of a flag, a judge's robes,
last Wednesday's sunset, blood at the dentist's, flamingoes,
garnets, a pillar box, fuchsia, morocco leather,
a pimpernel? What is selected will of course
isolate you for nobody includes the same
objects in a suitcase. Only music perhaps
can command the logic of its ingredients.
Wherever painting is involved the room,
the air dictate their gold, their mistiness. Glitter
of flood-water gets into the simplest paragraph
of a letter home so how can a poet say what is
or is not present in his poem. Fixing the terms
is the first task though organised with dangers
like opening windows on the cold side of a house.

The Third Elegy

Reality never gets into the newspapers.
A snapshot or a television programme
are most remarkable for what they leave out.
Swann said, "They call our attention each day
to insignificant things whereas we read
three or four times in our life the books in which
lie the essentials." Outlines of metaphor
rest on the map and the rain falling so quietly
is not the real rain. Water-lilies bloom now
in the pool, wax-yellow, scarlet. The dragonfly
we saw yesterday darts, a bronze flash among reeds,
and I stroll twice a day down to the post office
and collect nothing. None of this is correct
though the truth is present as a tight bead of water
among the hard petals. You took me by the hand
and told me of your unhappiness. No phrase,
no caress of mine reached the boundary of sadness,
altered it. This won't work either though reality
sometimes occurs in a poem just as it's only
in examination of time that eternity
makes any sense. If on a journey you stay
obsessed with the contents of your pockets
you will not be touched by the development of space
and space is the protection of the infinite.
The bird sang deep in the forest, the horseman
galloping up the ride did not hear its call
though later that evening when the rain held off
the crescents punched by the hooves brimmed with water
and perhaps the same bird went flying across
its own reflection. Wonder is a faculty
many do their utmost to smother in children
but when the pear drops on wet grass and the moon
urges the tide among salt-flats, the world

declares its magic the way in the silent garden
the figure walking by the tall box-hedge
was not there at the turn in the path. Two people
in love who share the same interests — films, coins, wine —
disagree over the method of pruning roses
and fascination with cut glass or prehistory
may appear uninviting. But poetry
is neither a pastime nor a public act.
It is an ordering and from that rearrangement
each reader extracts another. In among
the gestures of the orchestra a music emerges
that was not the composer's intention.
You can train the intellect as you would a retriever
or a sheep-dog but it is only one of many
apprehensions — there are also the five
senses, instinct a sixth one, emotions forming
a barrier like intolerance or else a dye
like joy, a soul that teaches us to love
and the spirit, atrophied in many, that holds
relations outside time. It is as absurd
to limit response to reason as to obey
a tone-deaf man's view of a concert.
I do not try hard enough to see through your eyes.
And I know, dear, I bore you. Once, years ago,
an archer entered the mews where dusty windows
brought in the morning and hooded falcons
gripped their perches. He chose ten arrows.
Dew glistened on the short grass for the hay
had been stacked the week before. He set the target
clear against the darkness of the forest.
Stringing his bow he shot the arrows one by one
which missed the padded circle and stuck like a grove
of leafless saplings bent by the wind. How else
can I define my love as the words employed
replace my passion with the unreal events
of metaphor? How may I leave my love for you

fixed on the fields of time if I can't
convey the unspoken except with words.
Others have painted the conquest of death and shown
the calm Christ stepping over the sprawled soldiers.
Others depicted the blaze of recognition in the inn
as the travellers grasp the fact they've been walking
along the edge of two worlds. Reality lies
in the empty tomb, on the road to Emmaus.
What will convince you that this is not blasphemy?
Love must go beyond the here and now
if it is to be anywhere. I think I tried
to read the misery in your eyes that day.
When you cross a familiar room in the darkness
the table you do not brush against is still there.

The Fourth Elegy

The starting-point may once have been a rose
or a rose-seed or, as you watch through glass
burnished by autumn, one petal falling
and striking the thorns as it falls. An age
of lyricism can be said to have ended.
He stands there, flushed and starlit before the mirror,
uttering cryptic phrases, for instance, "The well
is fed by a spring on the highest point of the island"
and the reflection laughs back with Arcturus
studding the bare shoulder. The finest of all
influences is memory. Zophar, the third
of Job's comforters, says of the secrets of wisdom
that they are double to that which is.
A new enigma is detected gliding
under the surface of words where dark alders
hang low and insects form a dancing cloud.
There are times when no phoenix rises screeching
from its charred nest and the day leads dry
and unconsoling in every direction.
In exile however he gets up early,
breakfasts alone by the sunny window and watches
the lines of snow-capped peaks above the pine-trees
forming the frontier, for here they speak a different language.
He spends each morning at work on his masterpiece.
His hosts are considerate — he has this house
rent-free plus an income. And he is at liberty.
At evening, alone, a sense of pointlessness
enfolds him like smoke. Why pin any hope on the next
generation or on the next but two?
Those who might find these pages scorched with his indignation
of interest, even of use, are distant and timorous.
Sales of his work in translation grow less every year.
He was once a wonder, his books, his integrity

valuable fodder for speeches on freedom
but now it's the tenth day and the world has changed.
This cool gallery is lined with ancestors
of a total stranger, some in armour, some in orange velvet,
proud or stupid or handsome, having one thing in common,
the gift of death. To pass dutifully before each portrait
is little good. One is sometimes in too much of a hurry
even to examine the curl of a peony,
the gleam of light on a far pond or the cloud
whose summer brightness holds a dark blur of rain.
A glint of silver among the shadows of rosewood
recalled that room, do you remember? and the sunset
lighting the end of the street while the high gulls
drifted. The questioner remains austere
in the very centre of recollection. Logic
must never be ignored but cannot equal
conviction like a radiance behind the eyelid.
At rare moments of revelation there is only
the state of being as foliage is in gold air.
I know because I can't be sure, I am aware
but locked in rings of iridescence that conceal
time. There are two kingdoms. You belong in both, the one
where you degenerate and where all paths
must peter out in grass or stone or other paths
and the other where the moment stands
weightless in splendour. The platform was empty.
Milk churns were stacked in the warm shadow.
A smell of haycocks came from the near field
and a score of caged pigeons waited murmuring
for their release. When evening comes you sit
reading and the book falls to your lap and the corn
left by the harvesters sways with ripeness.
Or I watch you sleeping. Every frontier
is made up of such moments. It is a question
never of place but of time. The mirror as well
holds danger especially when, fringed with dusk,

a white face flickers behind you, vanishes.
The future too has barriers between room and room
but at times it is enough to write letters
as the moon's course slants across the square of window
and offer a few friends who may never read them
the chance of sharing in a borrowed midnight.

The Fifth Elegy

Airs of summer wind their way through the empty chamber
for the skulls have gone to stare behind glass at a crude
map on the museum wall. Perhaps the bones
were removed piecemeal when the mound fell in. The sun is low
and slopes of tough grass fleeced with hazel
repeat the fragrance of the day. High stone slabs
freed from burial by five thousand years of rain
stand in the light and frost. You do not like these journeys.
Along a green-sided estuary where the tides race
hedgerows are twined with dogrose and stunted
apple-trees crowd against the white-washed farmhouse.
Fuchsia blooms by the gate until late November.
Beyond the water, fields lift towards the sunset where bare rocks
are whipped by the fog. The ferry would take us dryshod
past a brown seagull floating. The brasswork shines,
flush with the fine red wood. Each screw is countersunk.
Blue leather cushions are spotless and the rowlocks
turn silently. Art matters as itself, as structure,
as joy in its own structure though the function
may be to get something across. You must remain
conscious of the surface, its music, the promise
of another world even when the devil is muttering
lacklustre words. The worst is to be tempted not to try.
Better to scoff forbidden fruit than offer
the easel for sale. You can't make money the way
you make a sonata, make a field give grain,
make love, unless the coins are counterfeit.
The unimportant aspects last each day
from nine to five. It was a still June evening.
The guests stood by the open window. When they'd gone in
to dinner, glancing round the table, she asked
my cousin where the grey lady had gone, the one
all by herself in the other room. And her host warned her

by kicking her under the table for the grey
lady was seldom seen indoors, preferring it seemed
narrow paths of the garden, the scent of stocks
and warm brown bees working among the lavender.
Old houses like churches find it hard to exclude
the bruises of memory and layers of atmosphere
placed there by prayer or perhaps incidentally
because of a quarrel never properly made up —
year after year some grudge against destiny,
letters unsealed that glowed with stale
impressions from abroad. You'll find a lace fan
and a jigsaw in that cabinet — also
a pack of cards with the nines missing. Sculling
on a foreign lake the son who'd sold the estate
heard distinctly the stable-clock chiming. There's a green
cul-de-sac lined with the graves of dogs. The hill
looks over glittering beech-trees to the moor.
You climbed a different path, one that seemed easier,
and we met by a bed of yellow roses
twisted by the wind. The children were there already
pretending to be horses. We saw the white half-moon
and the distant colours of the sea. Naturalism
is an outmoded form. For a millennium
those who were buried in the shadow of that church-tower
have known of life what we know, that reason
reaches only so far before the truth
takes over. Listen now to the first birdcall
as the trees show a barely perceptible
shiver of green. And water too is sacred in well
and trough and font like hawthorn-leaves and the red
cord that links the child to the mother. You struggled
slipping on greasy chalk in the lane that autumn
and your beauty, flushed, laughing, was such that my heart
was seized with more love than I had imagined possible.
Who though can put a face on words or claim
to interpret the sundial? All we can say for certain is

there was a house, a tomb, a copse, and beyond
the land sloped to the river-mouth. This journey
will take its place among the many ways
of identifying movement. The portraits have arrived.
So have your books. Look at the distance. It has been
a cold summer. I was told in the village this morning
that the old man who rowed the ferry has died.
We could hire a car and drive inland to the bridge.
It's not on this map but would you like to go?

The Sixth Elegy

The track, cut in the yellow stone, runs straight
between flowering shrubs. To the left the ground drops,
the trickle of a stream is clearly audible. The southern sky
is hidden by the slope of trees, green upon green,
swaying. On the path it's still, sheltered from the wind.
In one room only, though at frequent intervals,
the furniture was shifted, usually at night,
but not always. This is a fairly well-known
phenomenon — like the spare needles
twisted out of shape inside the sewing-machine
or the pair of scissors found in the empty scullery
with a black zigzag running the length of one blade.
The horse was discovered kicking, terrified,
in a disused room with a door so narrow
they had to break down a wall to get him out.
Puberty seems to provide a focus for these storms
almost as if the child hitherto controlled
by other forces trembles between two
contradictory poles. One often uses 'it'
for a child and perhaps absolute possession
of gender, fixing the young man or woman,
atrophies other powers. What was glimpsed, once, no longer,
between the fickle leaves? A king and queen,
their naked bodies the colour of wild flowers,
stroll laughing and the sound of their laughter
is shrill, anarchic. A fairy huntsman pursues
the unwitting adult and transfixes his head
with a silver lance that vanishes. A tall figure
created itself out of dancing shadows and moved
across the wood like details of another wood.
The house shook slightly. If you treat the symbol
as a screen before an object claiming the thorn
indicates protection or the ruined barn

the failure of the old ideas you reduce the painting
to a work in code. The hills of allegory are real
hills, stars burn and the lion stalks among high trees
lashing its tail. It is often an effort
to look north and south among the images
and those who translate the poem into prose
are praised for having found the solution
for the achievements of intellect are the ones
that seem to count. Lip-service paid to dead poets
or to the statements of religion is as much as most
are prepared to pay. But Blake not alone knew
it's the other way round. What the narrow-minded
conceive of as reality is only the first step.
We have lived elsewhere. How otherwise explain
the shock of recognition at the gap in the hedge,
that day high on the downs when the sun led you
to a place you knew though it was your first visit.
Each dawn renews our loss. Half-creatures, stumbling,
seeing through a divided eye, we slip
from plane to plane and walk bewildered as the light
rises and shifts the distances round until
we are uncertain of our whereabouts and wonder
which one is our companion, which the ghost.
The cuckoo flew hooting above the rowan-tree
where the stone avenue points downhill to the spring
that trickles from the grass. You have seen this
and gone over marshy ground in winter to find
the last brooklime unshrivelled and the crow's
shadow on a litter of bones. The danger
lies not in loneliness but in absorption
leading to self-absorption. This was never meant.
There is the need to be kissed and the need
to be by oneself. Our children called out in sleep
and my own nightmare put the wrong faces on friends.
No comfort issues from the dark. There is a splendour
inside the heart that cannot be challenged.

Who is that pale woman with grey hair standing silent in the white room? She smiles as though she recognised who we are. The moat is frozen, the orchard stark and bare. If we are patient there won't be time for questions at the end.